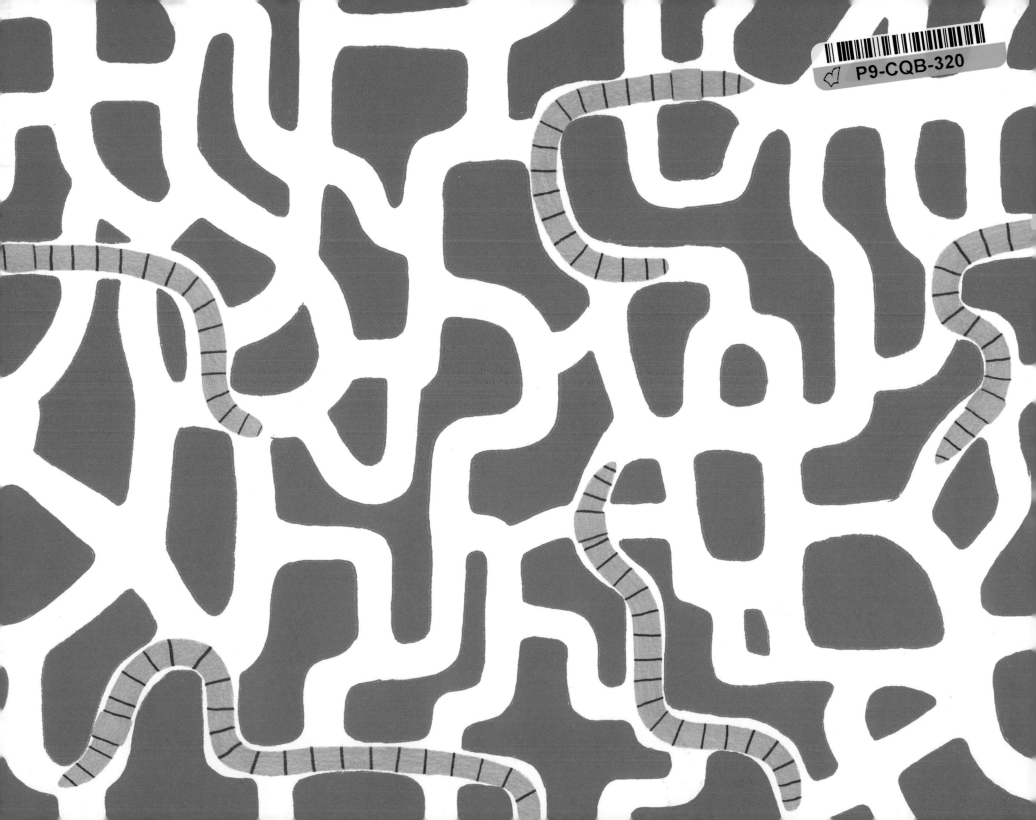
P9-CQB-320

This Is a BOOK to READ with a WORM

Ready?

Jodi Wheeler-Toppen

Illustrated by Margaret McCartney

Charlesbridge

For Violet and Jack—J. W.-T.

For worm scientists Mac and Roberto!

For my two sweetie pies, Jeff and Felix—M. M.

Text copyright © 2020 by Jodi Wheeler-Toppen
Illustrations copyright © 2020 by Margaret McCartney

All rights reserved, including the right of reproduction in whole or in part in any form. Charlesbridge and colophon are registered trademarks of Charlesbridge Publishing, Inc.

At the time of publication, all URLs printed in this book were accurate and active. Charlesbridge, the author, and the illustrator are not responsible for the content or accessibility of any website.

Published by Charlesbridge
85 Main Street
Watertown, MA 02472
(617) 926-0329
www.charlesbridge.com

Library of Congress Cataloging-in-Publication Data
Names: Wheeler-Toppen, Jodi, author. | McCartney, Margaret, illustrator.
Title: This is a book to read with a worm / Jodi Wheeler-Toppen; illustrated by Margaret McCartney.
Description: Watertown, MA : Charlesbridge, [2020]
Identifiers: LCCN 2018032575 (print) | LCCN 2018035950 (ebook) | ISBN 9781632897701 (ebook) | ISBN 9781632897718 (ebook pdf) | ISBN 9781580898973 (reinforced for library use)
Subjects: LCSH: Earthworms—Juvenile literature. | Naturalists—Juvenile literature.
Classification: LCC QL391.A6 (ebook) | LCC QL391.A6 W4985 2019 (print) | DDC 592/.64—dc23
LC record available at https://lccn.loc.gov/2018032575

Printed in China
(hc) 10 9 8 7 6 5 4 3 2 1

Illustrations created in sumi ink and pencil and then colored and collaged in Photoshop
Display type set in Luella Basic 1 by Cultivated Mind Designs by C. M. Kinash
Text type set in Blauth by Sofia Mohr
Color separations by Colourscan Print Co Pte Ltd, Singapore
Printed by 1010 Printing International Limited in Huizhou, Guangdong, China
Production supervision by Brian G. Walker
Designed by Joyce White and Diane M. Earley

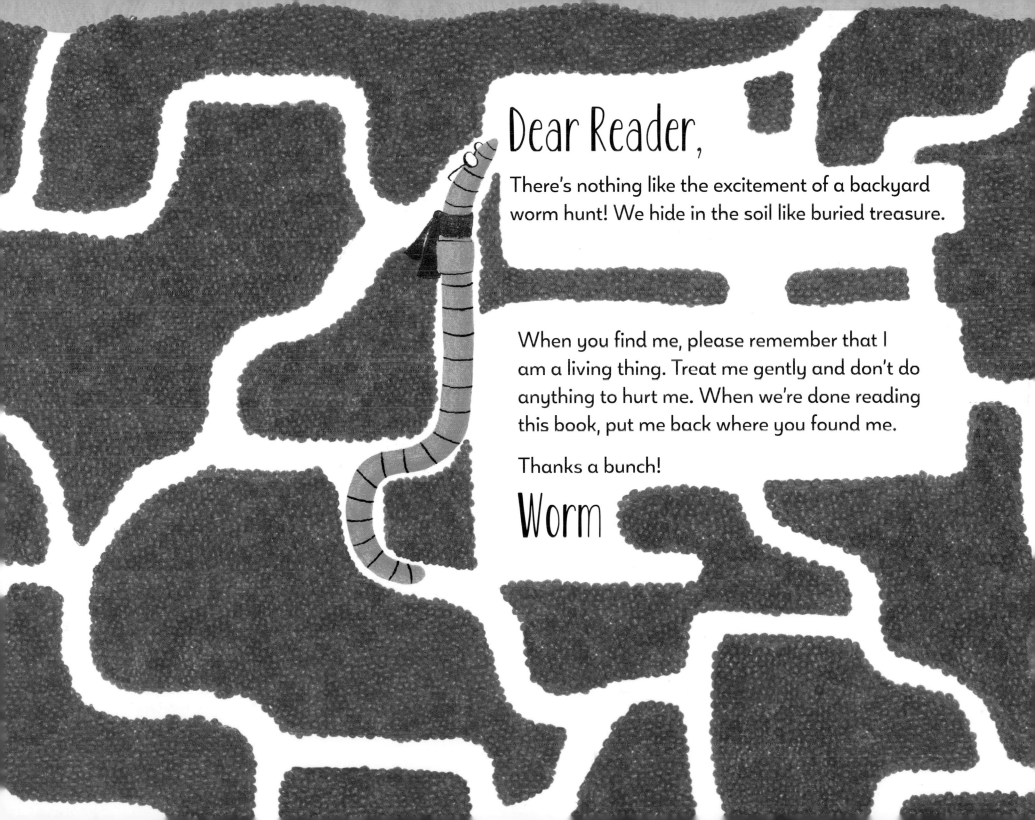

Dear Reader,

There's nothing like the excitement of a backyard worm hunt! We hide in the soil like buried treasure.

When you find me, please remember that I am a living thing. Treat me gently and don't do anything to hurt me. When we're done reading this book, put me back where you found me.

Thanks a bunch!

Worm

STOP! To read this book you are going to need a worm.

If you don't have one,
go outside to find one.
Look for a damp, leafy
spot and sift the leaf
layer for a hint
of wiggle.

Or grab a trowel,
scoop a pile of dirt, and
crumble it gently in your hand.

Or try pulling up a few large
weeds, roots and all. Some
worms hide in tangled root balls.

We'll also need water, paper
towels, a flashlight, a bottle
of rubbing alcohol, a cotton
swab, a sandwich bag, a sheet
of paper, a clear plastic bottle,
and aluminum foil.

Make your worm comfortable.

Pour some water on a paper towel and settle your new friend on top. Worms don't have lungs. They get oxygen through their wet skin.

You say it clih–TEL–lum or cly–TEL–lum.

Run your finger across your worm's back. Feel the **bump-bump-bump** as you slide across the rings. Is there a fat band over some of the rings?

This band is the **clitellum**. If your worm has one, then it is an adult. Otherwise, it's probably still a kid.

Feel free to give me a name. Just don't expect me to come when called.

Find your worm's head.

If you have an adult, this is easy. The head is the end closest to the clitellum. If you have a kid, you'll have to watch it move. Worms usually crawl headfirst.

Hold up your worm face-to-face. Not much of a face, is it? Can you find eyes? How about a nose?

Set your worm on the damp paper towel and shine a flashlight right at its head.

Look at it go!

Your worm doesn't have eyes, so it can't see shapes or colors. But it does have sensors that tell light from dark.

Bright, sunny places are filled with birds, mice, and snakes that would love to gobble up your worm. You can't blame your worm for preferring the dark.

Open a bottle of rubbing alcohol and take a small sniff. That's a strong smell! Can your worm smell it? Soak the end of a cotton swab in alcohol and hold it near— but not touching—your worm's head.

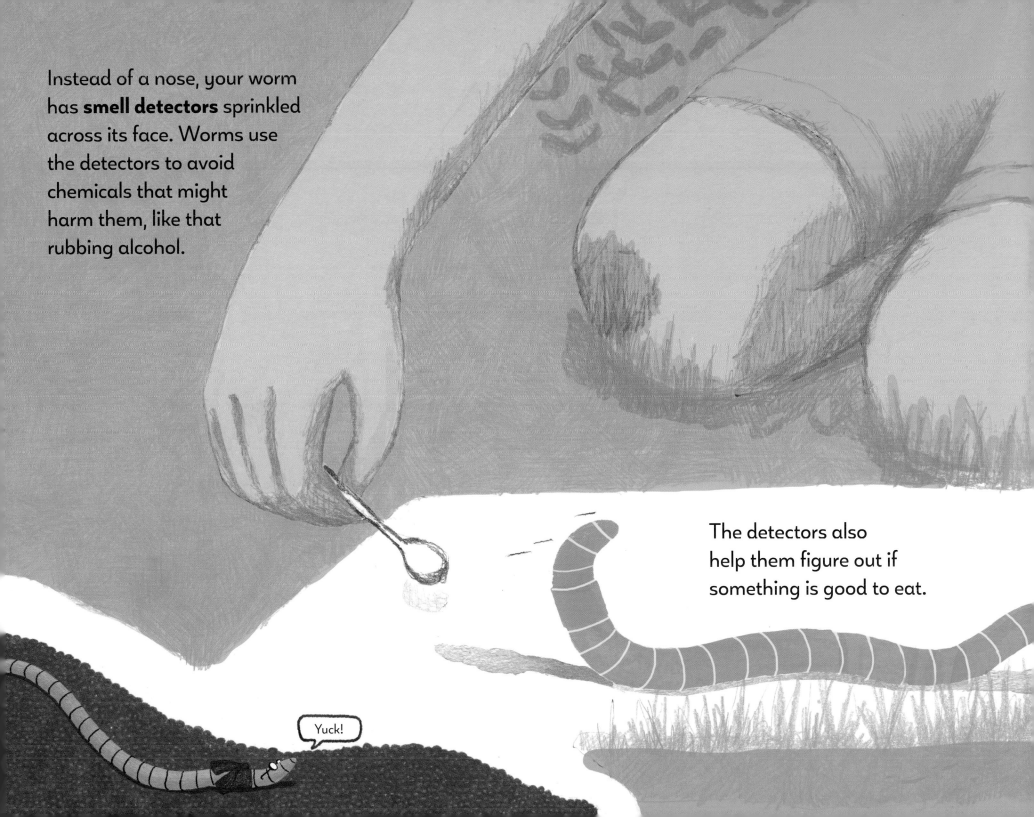

Instead of a nose, your worm has **smell detectors** sprinkled across its face. Worms use the detectors to avoid chemicals that might harm them, like that rubbing alcohol.

The detectors also help them figure out if something is good to eat.

Yuck!

Take another look at your worm's face. That hole is its mouth. Hey! Did it just stick its tongue out at you?

That's not really a tongue. Your worm has an organ called a **pharynx** just inside its mouth.

The pharynx sucks up soil, dead leaves, and rotting plants to eat. In some worms, the pharynx pokes through the mouth to grab food.

That's FER-inks or FA-rinks. Some worms keep their pharynx in their mouths, but it still does a fine job of pulling in tasty leaves.

Slip your worm
into a sandwich bag.
(But don't seal it—you
aren't taking a worm
for lunch!) Shine the
flashlight through
the back of the bag.

Ta-da!
You can see your
worm's digestive
system.

The dark clumps are
your worm's most
recent meal.

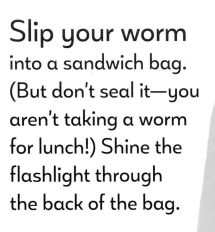

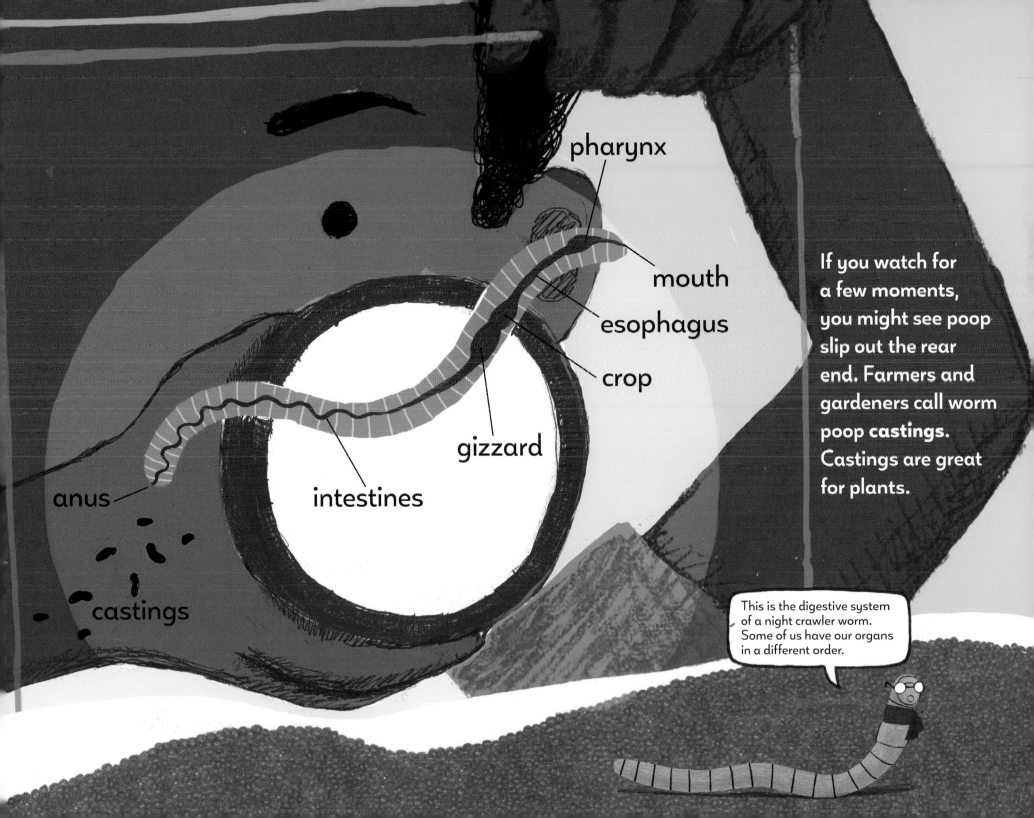

pharynx

mouth

esophagus

crop

gizzard

intestines

anus

castings

If you watch for a few moments, you might see poop slip out the rear end. Farmers and gardeners call worm poop **castings**. Castings are great for plants.

This is the digestive system of a night crawler worm. Some of us have our organs in a different order.

Take your worm out of the sandwich bag

and lay it back on the wet paper towel.

Gently tap it on the tail to get it moving and then try to copy its movements with your pointer finger.

Your finger doesn't make a very good worm, does it? You have bones in your finger, so it can only bend at the joints, where the bones meet up. Worms don't have bones. Their muscles attach to their skin, and they can bend at each segment, or ring, in their body.

A worm on the move

is constantly changing its shape. One moment, its front end looks like a short, fat sausage. Then it stretches out like a spaghetti noodle.

If you looked at your worm through a microscope, you would see that each segment has a few thin, stiff bristles, called **setae**. Your worm digs the setae on its front segments into the soil (or wet paper towel). The front setae hold on tight while your worm drags the back segments forward. Then it holds on with the back setae so it can push the front out, long and thin.

That's pronounced SEE-tee.

Setae are hard to see,
but you can hear them.

Roll a piece of paper into a
cone shape so it looks like
a megaphone.

Set your worm inside the fat
end of the cone, and hold the
small end to your ear.

Sit still and quiet. Do you hear
scratching in the tube? It comes
from the setae. Your worm is
trying (without much luck) to
anchor itself on the smooth paper.

Setae don't work well on paper,
but they are perfect for crawling through soil.
Give your worm some dirt, and let it spend
an entire night exploring.

Take a clean, clear plastic bottle and have
an adult cut away the top. Fill the bottle
with soil and leaf bits.

Welcome your wiggly friend to Hotel Worm,
and cover the entire container with
aluminum foil to block out
the light.

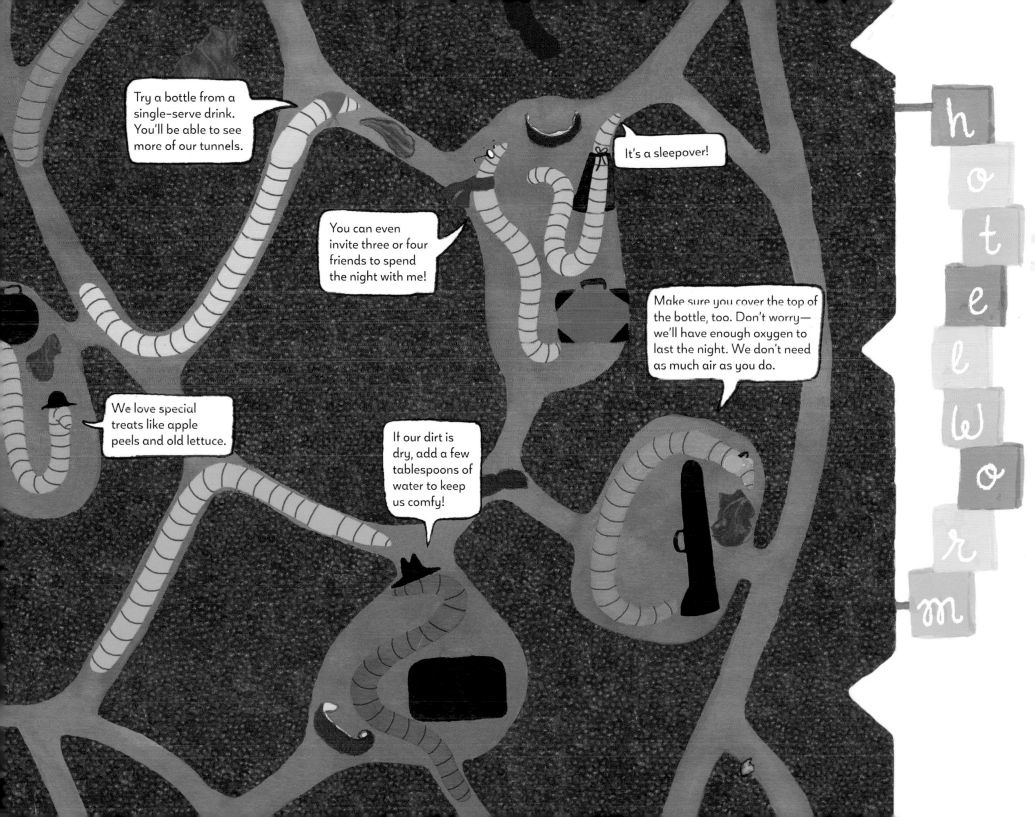

In the morning

peel back the aluminum foil and check out your worm's tunneling masterpiece! See how far you can trace the tunnels around the bottle.

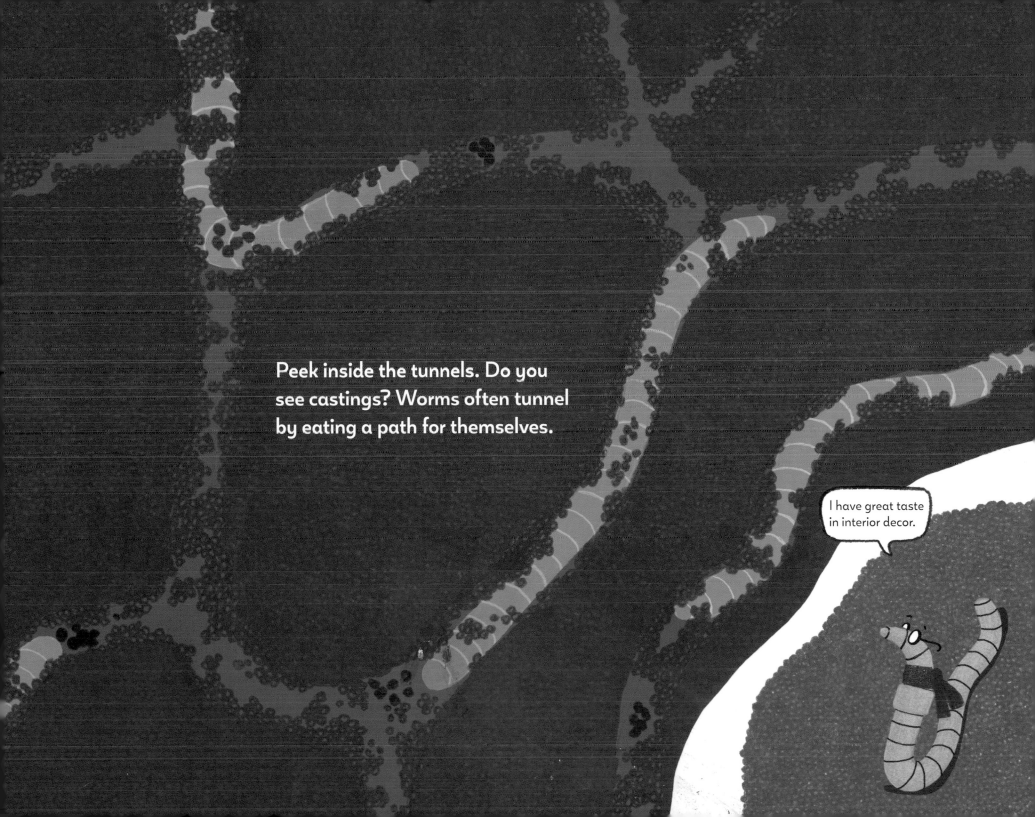

Peek inside the tunnels. Do you see castings? Worms often tunnel by eating a path for themselves.

It's time for your worm to go home.

Take the bottle back to the place where you found
your worm. Dump the dirt out, worm and all.

Before your worm slips away, bid it goodbye, wish it well, and thank it for helping you read this book.

Other Questions You May Have About Your Worm

What worm? I can't even find one!
When digging for worms be sure to pick a good spot.

Worms generally DON'T like:
- areas that are mostly sand or solid clay
- hot, dry dirt
- lawns that have been treated with pesticides or fertilizer

Worms DO like:
- areas with lots of leaves and dead plants on the ground
- loose soil
- cool, shady areas
- soil that is wet but not soaking

Worms will come to the surface in the morning and evening if the ground is wet enough. Try soaking the ground at dawn or dusk. Then come back in about twenty minutes to see who might have emerged.

If all else fails, you can buy worms at a bait shop. If you choose this option, please return them to the store or give them to a fisher friend when you are done. Believe it or not, non-native worms are taking over forests in some parts of the United States and eating so many leaves that other plants and animals don't have enough.

What kind of worm do I have?

Most people think a worm is just a worm, but there are over seven thousand species of earthworms. Scientists divide all those worms into three main groups, based on where they live. If your worm is reddish-brown and was found in a pile of leaves or in the dirt just below, you can be pretty sure you have an epigeic (eh-pih-JEE-ik) earthworm. These worms eat leaves above ground and don't build permanent burrows. Red wigglers are common epigeic earthworms.

If your worm is white, gray-blue, or yellowish and you dug into the dirt to get it, then you probably have an endogeic (en-doh-JEE-ik) worm. Endogeic worms make burrows in the top few layers of the soil, especially in areas with many plant roots. A common endogeic worm is the angleworm.

If your worm is over 6 inches (about 15 centimeters) long and you found it peeking out of its burrow, you probably have an anecic (uh-NEE-sik) worm, such as a night crawler. These worms build long burrows that go as deep as 6 feet (1.8 meters) underground. They come to the surface at night to grab leaves and drag them below the surface to dine.

On the other hand if you found your worm in Australia and it is even longer than you, you might have found a rare giant Gippsland earthworm. In that case put this book down and call your local worm scientists to report a sighting!

Do I have a baby worm?

Technically a baby worm is called a hatchling. Worms lay their eggs in rubbery, pea-sized sacs called cocoons. The cocoons look a bit like footballs minus the lacing.

When the hatchlings first come out, they are almost clear and can be thinner than spaghetti noodles.

But not all tiny worms are hatchlings! Many small worms are just that—small worms. If your worm has a clitellum, it's an adult, no matter how tiny it is.

Is my worm a boy or a girl?

Yes!

Your worm has ovaries that hold eggs. Eggs are what make an animal a female. For an egg to develop into a hatchling, it has to be joined with sperm. Your worm has that, too. The sperm makes it a male.

So your worm is a hermaphrodite, or an animal that is both male and female. In most species, it still takes two worms to make hatchlings. Each one gives the other some sperm and then wriggles off to lay eggs.

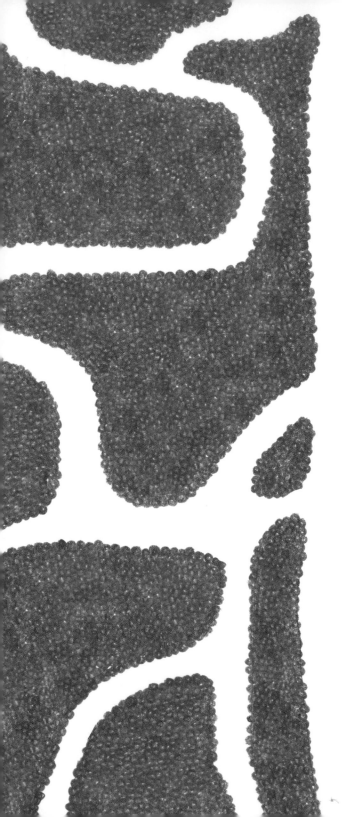

Further Resources

"The Adventures of Herman: The Autobiography of Squirmin' Herman the Worm." University of Illinois Extension, 2019.
https://extension.illinois.edu/worms/
Information about the history, classification, anatomy, habitat, and importance of earthworms. Includes games and activities.

Lunis, Natalie. *Wiggly Earthworms*. New York: Bearport, 2009.
Well-labeled photographs show hard-to-see details of earthworms.

McCloskey, Kevin. *We Dig Worms!* New York: TOON Books, 2015.
Fun worm information for new readers.

Pfeffer, Wendy. *Wiggling Worms at Work*. Illustrated by Steve Jenkins. New York: Harper Collins, 2004.
Detailed information and beautiful pictures.

Research Notes

I am extremely grateful to Mac Callaham, a US Forest Service research ecologist, and Roberto Carrera-Martínez, a PhD student at the University of Georgia's Warnell School of Forestry and Natural Resources, for spending most of a day talking worms with me. I also dug into two old but still solid research tomes: C. A. Edward and J. R. Lofty's *Biology of Earthworms* (London: Chapman and Hall, 1972) and Paul Hendrix's *Earthworm Ecology and Biogeography in North America* (Boca Raton, FL: Lewis, 1995). Online I found a wealth of useful information, including earthworm identification guides, at *Nature Watch: Worm Watch* (https://www.naturewatch.ca/wormwatch/) and its US partner, *Great Lakes Worm Watch* (http://www.greatlakeswormwatch.org).

The URLs listed here were accurate at publication, but websites often change. If a URL doesn't work, you can use the internet to find more information.